CompTIA A+

By Solis Tech

All-in-One Certification Exam Guide for Beginners!

2nd Edition

CompTIA A+ (2nd Edition): All-in-One Certification Exam Guide for Beginners!

Table of Contents

Introduction

I want to thank you and congratulate you for downloading the book, *"CompTIA A+: All-in-One Certification Exam Guide for Beginners!"*

This book contains proven steps and strategies on how to prepare for the CompTIA A+ exams.

This eBook will explain the basics of the CompTIA A+ certification and tests. It will also give you some pointers regarding the topics that you need to review. By reading this book, you will gain the knowledge and skills required to pass the tests.

Thanks again for downloading this book, I hope you enjoy it!

Chapter 1: The CompTIA A+ Examination

This eBook is written for people who are knowledgeable about computers. It assumes that you know to how to use a computer and its peripherals (e.g. printers, modems, etc.). This book will serve as your guide in preparing for the CompTIA A+ exam.

The A+ Certification

This is a certification program developed by CompTIA (Computer Technology Industry Association). This program is designed to provide a consistent way of checking the competency of computer technicians. The A+ certificate is given to people who have reached the degree of knowledge and diagnostic skills required to give proper support in the PC industry.

The A+ certification is similar to other programs in the industry (e.g. Microsoft Certified Systems Engineer and Novell's Certified Novel Engineer). The principle behind these certification programs is that if you need to get services for their products, you want to find technicians who have been certified by these programs.

The Benefits of Being A+ Certified

There are many reasons to get your own A+ certification. The information packet distributed by CompTIA gives the following benefits:

- It serves as a proof of your professional achievement.

- It improves your marketability.

- It gives you excellent advancement opportunities.

- It is now considered as a requirement for other kinds of advanced computer training.

- It encourages customers to do business with you

How to Become Certified

The A+ certification is given to anyone who passes the exams. You are not required to work for any company. CompTIA is not a secret group or society. It is, on the other hand, a group of elite computer technicians. If you want to be A+ certified, you have to do these things:

- Pass the exam called A+ Essentials

- Pass one of the three technician examinations:

    o IT Technician Test

- o Depot Technician Test

- o Remote Support Technician Test

You can take the tests at any Pearson VUE or Thompson Prometric testing center. If you will pass both exams, you will receive a mail from CompTIA. That letter will inform you that you passed the tests. Additionally, it contains the certificate, a lapel pin, and a business card.

How to Sign Up for the Exams

To sign up for the tests, you may call Pearson VUE at 1-877-551-7587 or register online at www.vue.com. For Thompson Prometric, call 1-800-777-4276 or visit the website www.2test.com.

These companies will ask for your name, employer, phone number, mailing address, and SSN (Social Security Number). If you don't want to give out your SSN, a provisional number will be given to you. Additionally, they will ask when and where you want to take the exam.

Obviously, the exams aren't free. You have to pay your chosen testing company. That means you have to specify the payment arrangement during the registration process. You can simply provide your credit card information to the customer representative you will talk to. If you're doing it online, you can enter the credit card info on their payment page.

Who Should Use This Book?

If you want to pass the A+ tests, and do it confidently, you should use this book as a guide for your preparations. The A+ Essentials test is created to measure basic skills for an entry-level computer technician. The technician tests are designed to certify that you have the required skills to service microcomputer hardware.

This eBook was created with one purpose in mind: to help you pass the A+ exams. This guide will do that by explaining the things on which you will be tested.

Chapter 2: The Different Parts of a Computer

A PC (i.e. personal computer) is a machine made up of different components that work together to perform tasks (e.g. helping you write a document or add up large numbers). With this definition, notice that computers are described as having various distinct parts that work together harmoniously. Nowadays, almost all computers are modular. That is, they possess parts that can be replaced if the owner wants to improve the performance of his device. Each part has a specific purpose. In this chapter, you'll learn about the parts that make up a common PC, how they work, and what their functions are.

Important Note: Unless stated otherwise, the terms "computer" and "PC" can be used interchangeably throughout this eBook.

The Different Parts of a Motherboard

The motherboard, also called the system or planar board, serves as the "spine" of a PC. This is the brown or green circuit board that you'll find at the bottom of your computer. The system board is the most important part of a PC since it houses and/or connects the other parts of a computer together.

Different Types of Motherboards

There are two main types of motherboards. These are:

Integrated Motherboards – With this type, most of the parts are integrated into the system board's circuitry. Basically, integrated motherboards are created for simplicity. Since majority of the components are already part of the board itself, you won't have to install them individually. However, this simplicity has a major drawback: once a component stops working, you cannot simply replace it; you have to replace the entire motherboard. These boards are cheap to manufacture but expensive to repair.

Note: If one of the parts breaks, you may just disable it and add an expansion card that has similar capabilities.

Nonintegrated Motherboards – Here, the major parts (e.g. disk controllers, video circuitry, etc.) are installed as expansion cards. You will easily identify this kind of system board since every expansion slot is occupied by a major component.

The Different Form Factors of Motherboards

Computer experts also classify motherboards according to their design (also known as *form factor*). Here are the main form factors being used today: NLX, BTX, ATX, and micro ATX. You have to be vigilant when buying a computer case and system board separately. Some cases lack flexibility: they might not accommodate the system board you will select.

Let's discuss each form factor:

1. NLX – This is the abbreviation for "New Low-profile Extended". In general, this form factor is used for cases that are low-profile. With this design, the expansion slots (e.g. PCI, ISA, etc.) are placed on a special card to reduce the vertical space they occupy. Daughter boards, or adapter cards, that are normally plugged vertically into the expansion slots, are placed parallel to the system board. That means their size won't affect that of the computer case.

2. BTX – This form factor was launched by Intel back in 2003. With this design, the head-producing parts are lined up against the power supply's exhaust fan and the air intake vents. Then, the other components are cooled by installing heat sinks on the motherboard. This design offers a quiet setup since it involves efficient airflow paths and fewer exhaust fans.

3. ATX – With ATX motherboards, the processor and memory slots form a 90° angle with the expansion cards. This design places the memory and processor in line with the power supply's exhaust fan. Thus, the processor can remain cool while it runs. In addition, you may add expansion cards (even the full-length ones) to an ATX motherboard since the memory and processor are not parallel to the expansion cards.

4. Micro ATX – This form factor is similar with the previous one, with one major difference: it is designed for smaller computer cases. Micro ATX motherboards benefit from the enhanced cooling designs of their full-sized counterparts. However, since they are smaller, they have lesser motherboard headers, integrated components, expansion slots, and memory modules.

Processors – Their Functions and Characteristics

Now that you are familiar with system boards, you have to learn about their most important part: the central processing unit (CPU). The CPU controls all of the computer's activities using both internal and external buses. Basically, it is a processor chip that contains millions of transistors.

Important Note: Nowadays, the word "chip" describes the whole package that a computer technician may install into a socket. However, this word was originally used to refer to the silicon wafer hidden inside the carrier (i.e. the "chip" you see on your motherboard). The pins that you see on the outer part of the carrier are connected to the silicon wafer's small contacts. These pins allow you to install the carrier into a socket.

You can identify which part inside the PC is the central processing unit: the CPU is a large square that lies flat on the motherboard with a large fan and heat sink.

The Features of Modern Processors

- Hyperthreading – This word refers to HTT (hyper-threading technology). Basically, HTT is a variant of SMT (simultaneous multithreading). This kind of technology uses the scalar architecture of modern CPUs.

  HTT-capable CPUs appear as two different processors to the computer's operating system (OS). Because of this, the OS may assign two processes simultaneously, such as symmetric multi-processing, where multiple processors utilize the same network resources. Actually, the OS should support SMP in order to use HTT. If a process fails because of missing information caused by, for instance, branch prediction problems, the processor's execution resources can be reassigned for a different procedure that can be conducted immediately. Thus, the processor's downtime is dramatically reduced.

- Multicore – A CPU that has a multicore design contains two processors inside the same package. Here, the OS may treat the CPU as if it were two different CPUs. Just like the HTT, the OS should support SMP. Additionally, SMP is not considered as an upgrade if the apps run on the SMP system are not meant for parallel processes. A good example for the multicore technology is the i7 Quad-Core Processor from Intel.

- Microcode – This is the group of instructions (also called instruction set) that compose the different microprograms that the CPU executes as it performs its functions. The MMX (multimedia extensions) is a special example of an individual microprogram that performs a specific instruction set. Basically, microcodes are at a lower level than the codes used in computer programs. On average, each instruction from a computer program requires a large number of microinstructions. Intel and other processor manufacturers incorporate the MMX instruction set into their products.

- Overclocking – This feature allows you to increase the performance of your CPU, on par with processors created to function at overclocked rates. However, unlike processors created to function on that speed, you have to make sure that the overclocked processor doesn't damage itself from the increased level of heat. You might need to install an advanced cooling system (e.g. liquid cooling) to protect the CPU and other computer parts.

- Throttling – Processor throttling, also called clamping, is the process that specifies the CPU time to be spent on a computer program. By specifying how individual programs use the processor, you can "treat" all of the applications fairly. The principle of Application Fairness turns into a major problem for servers, where each program may represent the work of another user. That means fairness to computer programs becomes fairness to the users (i.e. the actual customers). Customers of modern terminal servers take advantage of this feature.

Real World Example: CPU

If you want to know which processor your machine is using, you have to open the case and look at the numbers written on the CPU. This procedure requires you to remove the computer's heat sink. However, if you don't like to play around with computer parts, you may check the area around the processor. Some manufacturers place a sticker to provide information regarding the processor.

As an alternative, you may go online and visit the manufacturer's site. You just have to run a search for the model of your computer.

You may also right-click on "My Computer" and choose "Properties." The screen will show you a new window. Click on "General" and search for the "Processor" section. This part of the window will give you some details about your computer's processor. If you want to get more information, you may hit the "Start" button, click on "Accessories" and choose "System Tools."

Memory – Its Functions and Characteristics

Nowadays, memory is one of the easy, popular, and inexpensive methods to enhance a computer. While the computer's processor runs, it stores data in the machine's memory. Basically, the more memory a machine has, the faster it can operate.

To determine the memory of a computer, search for thin sets of small circuit boards that are packed together near the CPU. These circuit boards sit vertically on the computer's motherboard.

How to Check for Errors in a Computer's Memory

Parity Checking

This is a basic scheme used to check for errors. It lines up the computer chips in a single column and separates them into equal bit groups. These bits are numbered beginning at zero. All of the number x bits, one from every chip, create a numerical array. If you are using "even parity", for instance, you will count up the number of bits contained in the array. If the total number is even, you will set the parity bit to zero since the bit count is already even. If the total is an odd number, on the other hand, you should set the parity bit to 1 in order to even up the bit count.

This technique is effective in identifying the existence of errors in the arrays of bits. However, it cannot indicate the location of the errors and how to solve them. Keep in mind that this isn't error correction – it is just a simple error check.

ECC

ECC stands for *Error Checking and Correcting*. If the computer's memory supports this method, the system will generate and store check bits. Whenever the machine accesses its memory, an algorithm will be performed on the check bits. If the result turns out to be zero (or a group of zeros), the information contained in the memory is considered valid and the computer functions as normal. ECC can identify single-bit and double-bit errors. However, it can only correct errors that are single-bit in nature.

The Four Main Types of Memory

- DRAM – This is perhaps the most popular type of RAM out there. DRAM stands for *Dynamic Random Access Memory*. Because of their inherent simplicity, these memory chips are cheap and easy to create compared to the other types. This kind of memory is called dynamic since it needs constant update signals in order to keep storing the data written there. If the DRAM chips won't receive stable signals, the information they hold will be deleted.

- SRAM – This stands for *Static Random Access Memory*. Unlike DRAMs, this kind of memory doesn't require a steady stream of signals. In general, SRAM chips are more complex and expensive than DRAMs. You can use SRAM for cache functions.

- ROM – This is the abbreviation for Read-Only Memory. It is called as such because it prevents the user from editing the memory it contains. Once the data is written on the computer's ROM, it cannot be changed anymore. ROM is usually used to hold the machine's BIOS, since this data is rarely modified.

- CMOS – This is a special type of memory chip. It is designed to hold the configuration settings of a computer's BIOS. CMOS is battery-powered: that means the configuration is retained even if the machine is turned off.

Real World Example: Memory

Choosing the best memory for your computer is all about knowing the requirements of your CPU. In some cases, your motherboard decides which memory you should use. If you are using a cheap motherboard, a single-channel DDR2 can solve your problems. Modern motherboards, on the other hand, need DDR3 memory modules. This is 100% real "on paper." In the real world, however, high-end computer systems can also work with budget-friendly memory modules.

Let's assume that you went to a local store that sells computer parts a la carte. You want to set up a computer from scratch. In this example, let's say you have an Intel Core 2 processor. That processor has enough processing power (i.e. 3GHz), but you must use it with an LGA 775 socket. That means you have to spend a considerable amount of money to get excellent performance from your computer.

Additionally, this CPU requires DDR3 memory. You have to buy some modules with DDR3-1333 memory chips, particularly if you want to use a motherboard that is compatible with multi-channel memory.

Storage Devices – Their Functions and Characteristics

Computers are useless if they can't store anything. Storage devices hold the information being used, as well as the programs and files the computer needs in order to function properly. In general, storage devices are classified according to their capacity, access time, and physical attributes.

HDD Systems

HDD stands for *Hard Disk Drive*. This storage device is also called hard disk or hard drive. Computers use HDDs to allow quick access to data as well as permanent storage. Typically, hard disks are found inside a computer.

An HDD system is composed of:

Controller – This component controls the storage. It knows how the drive functions, emits signals to the different motors inside the disk, and accepts signals from the sensors within the drive. Nowadays, hard disk manufacturers place the drive and controller in one enclosure.

Hard Disk – This acts as the physical warehouse for the data. HDD systems store data on little disks (about 3-5 inches in diameter) grouped together and kept inside an enclosure.

Host Adapter – This is the system's translator: it converts signals from the controller and hard disk to signals the computer can work with. Most modern motherboards have a built-in host adapter, allowing drive cable connection through board headers.

Floppy Drives

Floppy disks are magnetic storage devices that use plastic diskettes enclosed in a tough casing. Several years ago, floppy disks were used to easily transfer information from one computer to another. Nowadays, few people are using floppy disks because of their small capacity. DVD-ROMs and CD-ROMs have replaced floppy disks in storing and transferring digital information.

CD-ROM Drives

Modern computers use CD-ROM drives. These compact disks are virtually similar to those used in music recording. CD-ROMs allow you to store data for a long period of time. In general, these drives are read-only: you cannot erase or delete the data once it is stored on a CD. In addition, computers need to spend a longer time in "reading" CDs compared to internal hard drives. Why are these drives so popular?

Despite their drawbacks, CD-ROMs are used because they can store large files (about 650MB) and are extremely portable.

DVD-ROM Drives

This is the newest storage device to be used for computers. The DVD (i.e. digital video disc) technology is mostly used for entertainment purposes (e.g. home theater systems). DVD-ROMs are basically similar to the DVDs you use at home. Because of this, computers that are equipped with a DVD-ROM drive can play movies stored on a DVD.

However, DVD-ROMs are way much more useful when used for computers. Since they use newer technology, DVD-ROMs are better than CD-ROMs in terms of storage capacity. On average, DVDs can hold 4GB of data. That means DVD-ROMs are your best option if you are storing or distributing large files.

Important Note: CD-ROMs and DVD-ROMs have the same appearance. The single difference is the logo on the front of DVD drives.

Removable Storage Devices

Many years ago, the term "removable storage" meant something extremely different from what it means now. Tape backup is one of the old storage devices that can still be bought today. Modern computer users prefer the solid-state, random-access removable storage devices. In this section, you'll learn about tape backups and the new storage solutions.

Tape Backup

This is an old type of removable storage. A tape backup device can be installed externally or internally and utilize either an analog or digital magnetic tape to store data. In general, this kind of device can hold more information than other storage mediums. However, they are also one of the slowest in terms of data transfer rate. Because of these reasons, tape backup devices are mainly used for archived information.

13

Flash Memory

Before, random-access memory chips were only used to access and use data. But now, you'll find them in different physical sizes and storage capacities. Flash memory drives are considered as the best solid-state storage device available. The flash memory category includes SD (secure digital) and other memory cards, USB flash drives, and older detachable and non-detachable memory mechanisms. Each of these storage devices has the capability to store huge amounts of information.

Manufacturers of flash memory devices use revolutionary packaging (e.g. keychain attachments) for their products to provide easy transport options for their end-users.

Chapter 3: How to Work With Computer Parts Effectively

While taking the CompTIA A+ exam, you will answer questions regarding the installation, usage, and replacement of computer parts. This chapter will help you to review regarding those topics.

How to Install, Configure and Optimize Computer Parts

Aside from knowing the characteristics and functions of PC components, you also need to know how to use them. In particular, you should be familiar with the installation, configuration, and optimization of such parts.

How to Upgrade a Storage Device

Storage devices are available in different shapes and sizes. Aside from IDE and SCSI, two of the most popular types, there are SATA (Serial ATA) and PATA (Parallel ATA). You can also   differentiate between external and internal drives. This section of the book will explain each of these options.

Preparing the Drive

Regardless of the technology being used, you should format storage devices before using them. Although most drives have their own formatting software, each OS has a tool that you can use. When working with Windows computers, you can utilize the format utility through the command line. If you are working with XP, Vista, 7, or newer Windows system, you can also use the graphical utility program called Disk Management.

How to Work with IDE

Before, IDE (integrated drive electronics) drives were the most popular kind of computer hard drives. Although they are often linked to hard drives, IDE is more than just an interface for hard disks. It can also serve as the interface for different storage types such as Zip, DVD, and CD-ROM.

To install IDE drives, you should:

1. Set the slave/master jumper on the IDE drive.

2. Place the drive inside the drive bay.

3. Connect the cable for power-supply.

4. Link the ribbon cable to the motherboard and to the drive.

5. If the drive isn't detected automatically, you should configure it using the BIOS Setup of your computer.

6. Use your PC's operating system to format and partition the IDE drive.

How to Work with SCSI

SCSI is the abbreviation for *Small Computer System Interface*. This kind of device can be either external or internal to the machine. To configure an SCSI device, you should assign an SCSI ID (also called SCSI address) to all of the devices in the SCSI bus. You can configure their numbers using a jumper or DIP switch.

Whenever the computer sends data to the SCSI device, it emits a signal on the cable assigned to that number. The device will respond with a signal that holds the device's number and the information needed.

You should install a terminator (i.e. terminating resistor device) at the two ends of the bus to keep the SCSI devices working. You can activate and/or deactivate terminators using a jumper.

Here are the things you should do when installing an SCSI device:

- For Internal Devices – Connect the cable (i.e. a 50-wire ribbon cable with multiple keyed connectors) to the adapter and to each SCSI device in your computer. Afterward, place the terminators on the adapter and terminate the final device in the chain. You should leave other devices unterminated.

- For External Devices - Follow the steps outlined above, but here, you should use some stub cables between the SCSI devices in the daisy chain (instead of a long cable that has multiple connectors). Terminate the adapter as well as the final device in the daisy chain (that device should have one stub cable linked to it).

- For Hybrid Devices – Many types of adapters have connectors for external and internal SCSI devices. If you have this kind of adapter, attach the ribbon cable to your internal devices and connect the cable to your adapter. Afterward, daisy-chain the external devices from the external port. Terminate the device at the end of every chain. Make sure that the adapter is unterminated.

External Storage Devices

As capacities shoot up and prices fall down, the number of available external storage devices has increased greatly. Aside from the SCSI variant explained above, you will also see devices with USB connections and those that can connect straight to the system. The computer's operating system will recognize USB devices upon connection. You can just install any additional programs you like to use. A computer program called Dantz Retrospect is included in many storage devices to allow you to utilize external devices as automatic backups.

If the external storage device is linked straight to the system, you can just follow the instructions that came with that product. Then, install additional programs on the computers that you will be using. The main benefit of linking straight to the system is that the storage device/s can be accessed by all of the computers.

How to Upgrade Display Devices

Before linking or unlinking a display device (e.g. a computer monitor), make sure that the computer and the device itself are powered off. Afterward, connect a cable from the computer's video card to the display device. Connect the power cord of that device to an electrical outlet. You may use a modern Digital Visual Interface (DVI) cable or the traditional DB-15 (or VGA) cable.

While installing a new monitor, you should have the proper driver. The driver is the software interface between the display device and the computer's OS. If you don't have the right driver, your monitor won't display what you want to see. Nowadays, you can download the newest drivers from the website of monitor manufacturers.

Aside from the power supply, the most dangerous part to repair is the monitor. Computer technicians say that beginners should never attempt to repair monitors. Monitors can hold high-voltage charges even if they have been powered off for several hours. That means you can be electrocuted if you will try to repair a monitor by yourself. If your monitor stopped working, and you don't want to buy a new one, you should take that device to a TV repair shop or a certified computer technician. The technicians and the repair guys know how to fix monitors properly – they understand the dangers and the correct procedures.

How to upgrade Input and Multimedia Devices

The typical upgrade for input devices is the transition to newer mice and keyboards.

Keyboards

Keyboards may wear out if used repeatedly. The usual problem is "key sticking", where keys are no longer responding to the user. To replace a PS/2 101-key keyboard with a new one, just unplug the old keyboard and plug in the new. As you can see, this is a quick and easy process. Nowadays, however, computer users prefer to replace old keyboards with USB ones.

Here is a principle you need to remember: You can use the "unplug-the-old-and-plug-in-the-new" procedure as long as your computer's OS supports the keyboard you want to use.

Mice

Computer mice also wear out because of repeated use. But don't worry: you can replace old mice with new ones. You may easily replace a PS/2 connection mouse

17

with another without spending too much. As an alternative, you may buy an optical mouse (which prevents dust- and ball-related problems) or a wireless one (which needs batteries to send and receive signals). Although new mouse models still use the PS/2 type of connection, most mouse products in the market use the USB connection.

Chapter 4: The Tools Needed for Checking Computer Parts

The CompTIA A+ exam will also test your skills in checking computer parts. This chapter will help you with that topic by discussing the tools and diagnostic procedures needed.

The Tools Needed by a Computer Technician

A great computer technician needs a great collection of tools. If you are working alone, you may not get past the troubleshooting phase. However, you still need to use certain tools in order to succeed in that task. Once you have identified the problem, you will need to get another set of tools in order to fix it.

This book will focus on the "hardware" tools. These are:

- Screwdrivers – When checking a computer technician's toolkit, you will surely find screwdrivers. Almost all of the big computer parts you'll see today are mounted using screws. If you need to remove these parts, you need to have the right type of screwdriver. This kind of tool is divided into three types:

    o Flat-Blade – Many people refer to this as the *common* or *standard* screwdriver. The screw used with this screwdriver is rarely used today (mainly because the screw's head can be destroyed easily).

    o Phillips – This is perhaps the most popular type of screwdrivers being used today. The screws used with a Phillips screwdriver have enough head surface: you can turn them many times without damaging the screws' head. According to recent reports, more than 90% of the screws used in computers belong to the Phillips-head type.

    o Torx – This is the type of screwdriver you use while working on tiny screws found on Apple and Compaq computers. The screws you remove using a Torx screwdriver have the most surface to work against: they offer the best resistance in terms of screw-head damage. Nowadays, Torx-type screws are gaining more popularity because of their clean and technical look.

- Flashlight – This is one of the tools you should always have. You'll realize how important this tool is when you're crawling under a table searching for a dropped computer part.

- Needle-Nose Pliers – You should have this in your toolkit. This kind of pliers is great for holding connectors or tiny screws (particularly if you have large hands). If needle-nose pliers are still too big to do certain tasks, you may use a pair of tweezers.

- Compressed Air – While working on a computer, you will usually remove the machine's case first. Once the cover is removed, it would be great if you will clean the computer's internal components. The clumps of dirt and fibers can block airflow inside the system unit. As a result, the PC's life will be shortened. The ideal way to eliminate the dust is by using compressed air.

  If you are working for a big company, you probably have a core air compressor that supplies compressed air. If this kind of compressor is not available, you may purchase canned compressed air. However, you'll be shelling out large amounts of money – cans of compressed air are expensive.

- Soldering Iron – You can use it to splice broken wires. Nowadays, computer technicians rarely use this tool. Here's the reason: modern computer parts are created with quick-disconnect connectors. You can easily replace them without splicing anything.

- Wire Strippers – Whenever you have to solder something, you need to use a stripper/wire cutter to prepare the wires for connection. Stripping means you will expose a certain part of the wire by removing the insulation.

- Multi-Meters – This tool is named as such because it is basically a set of different types of testing meters, such as ammeter, voltmeter, and ohmmeter. When used by a trained technician, a multi-meter can identify the failure of various types of computer parts.

  A multi-meter has an analog or digital display, a mode selector switch, and two probes. You can use the switch to perform two things: (1) select the function you want to test and (2) choose the range in which the meter will work. If you need to use an old meter to measure a power pack, you should manually set the range selector. Modern multi-meters, particularly the digital ones, can automatically find the correct ranges.

  Important Note: You should never measure voltage by connecting a manual ranging multi-meter to an AC electrical outlet. This will damage the meter itself, the meter mechanisms, or both.

How to Measure Resistance Using a Multi-Meter

Resistance is the property of electricity commonly measured when troubleshooting computer parts. This electrical property is measured in ohms and represented by the Greek letter "omega." If a multi-meter indicates infinite resistance, the electric currents cannot travel from one prove to another. If you are using a multi-meter to check the resistance and you are getting an infinite reading, there's a huge possibility that the wire is broken.

When measuring resistance, you should set the tool to measure ohms. You can do it using either the selector dial or the front button. Then, connect the PC component you want to measure between the tool's probes. The multi-meter will then show the component's resistance value.

How to Measure Voltage Using a Multi-Meter

This process is similar to the one discussed above, but with two main differences:

1. While measuring voltage, make sure that you properly connect each probe to the source of electricity. For DC voltage, the "-" should be connected to the negative side and the "+" to the positive one. This positioning is irrelevant when measuring AC voltage.

2. You should switch the selector to Volts DC (VDC) or Volts AC (VAC), depending on what you need to measure, to instruct the tool about the voltage you are working with. These settings protect the tool from overload. The multi-meter will blow up if you will plug it into a power source while it's still on "measure resistance" mode.

Chapter 5: Operating Systems

The CompTIA A+ examination will test your knowledge regarding operating systems. Since operating systems play an important role in the computer industry, you should be familiar with them. This chapter will guide you in this topic. Here, you'll learn different things about a computer's OS.

What is an Operating System?

Computers are useless if they don't have any piece of software. Well, you can use them as a doorstop or paperweight – but that is not cost-efficient. You need to have an interface before you can use the capabilities of a computer. And, if you don't know yet, software acts as the interface. Although there are different kinds of software, or computer programs, the most important one you'll ever need is the OS.

Operating systems have various functions, most of which are extremely complex. However, two functions are critical:

1. Interfacing with the computer's hardware

2. Providing an environment in which other pieces of software can run.

Here are the three main types of software that you will encounter in the CompTIA exam:

- Operating System – It provides a stable environment for other computer programs. In addition, it allows the user to enter and execute commands. The operating system gives the user an interface so they can enter commands (i.e. input) and get results or feedback (i.e. output). For this, the OS should communicate with the PC's hardware and conduct the tasks below:

    o Device access

    o Output format

    o Memory management

    o File and disk management

Once the operating system has performed these basic tasks, the user can enter instructions to the computer using an input device (e.g. a mouse or keyboard). Some of the commands are pre-installed in the operating system, whereas others are given using certain applications. The OS serves as the platform on which the PC's hardware, other pieces of software, and the user work together.

- Application – This is used to complete a specific task. Basically, an application is a computer program written to support the commands given to the OS. Every application is compiled or configured for the operating system it will be used for. Because of this, the application depends on the OS to perform most of its basic functions.

  When a program accesses the computer's memory and linked devices, it sends a request to the OS. The machine's operating system will perform the requests made by the program being used. This setup helps greatly in decreasing the programming overhead, since most of the executable codes are shared – they are written onto the operating system and can be used by different applications installed on the computer.

- Driver – This is an extremely specific program created to instruct an operating system on how to access and use a piece of hardware (e.g. webcam, flash memory, etc.). Every webcam or flash memory has distinct features and settings – the driver helps the OS in knowing how the new hardware works and the things it can do.

The Terms and Concepts Related to Operating Systems

In this section, let's define some of the most important terms and concepts. Study this section carefully since it will teach you the terms you'll encounter during the CompTIA A+ exam.

Key Terms

- Source – This is the code that explains how computer programs work. An operating system can be open source or closed source.

  o Open Source – The users have the right to change and examine the code.

  o Closed Source – The users are not allowed to edit or check the code.

- Version – This is a specific variant of a computer program, usually expressed by a number, which informs users regarding the "newness" of the software. For instance, MS-DOS is now in its sixth main version. Computer programmers distinguish minor revisions from major ones this way:

  o "Program" 4.0 to "Program" 5.0 is a major revision.

  o "Program" 5.0 to "Program" 5.2 is a minor revision.

- Shell – A piece of software that works on top of the operating system. It allows users to execute commands through an array of menus or a different type of graphical interface. A shell makes an operating system simpler and easier to use by modifying the GUI (graphical user interface).

- GUI – The method by which a user communicates with computers. A GUI uses a touchpad, mouse, or a different mechanism (aside from a keyboard) to interact with the machine and issue commands.

- Multithreading – The capability of a computer program to contain several requests in the computer's CPU. Since it allows an application to perform different tasks simultaneously, computers experience a boost in performance and efficiency.

- Network – A group of computers that are connected by a communication link. A network allows computers to share resources and information.

- Preemptive Multitasking – This is a multitasking technique in which the operating system allocates each program a certain amount of CPU time. Afterward, the OS takes back the control and provides another task or program access to the CPU. Basically, if a computer program crashes, the operating system takes the processor from the faulty program and gives it to the next one (which must be working). Even though unstable computer programs still get locked, only the affected application will stop – not the whole machine.

- Cooperative Multitasking – This is a multitasking technique that relies on the applications themselves. Here, each program is responsible for utilizing and giving up access to the CPU. Windows 3.1 used this method to manage multiple programs. If an application stalls while it is using the CPU, the application fails to free the CPU properly, and the whole computer gets locked, the user needs to reboot the machine.

Chapter 6: Power Supply

Without power, the components of a computer won't work. The part of the computer that gives the needed power is called "power supply." Basically, a power supply is a device that converts AC currents into DC voltages that computers need.

Important Note: A power supply contains capacitors and transformers that may discharge dangerous amounts of electricity. That means you have to be careful when working with this device, even if it has been unplugged for several hours. Power supplies are not meant to be repaired, especially by inexperienced personnel. It would be best to just replace bad power supplies with new ones.

Manufacturers rate power supplies in "watts" (i.e. a unit for measuring power). High watt numbers mean more power for your computer. You should consider the watt number as the device's capacity to provide power. Modern computers need power supplies with 200 to 500 watts.

Traditional power supplies use three kinds of connectors to provide electricity: (1) AT system connectors, (2) standard power connectors, (3) and floppy drive connectors. Each kind of connector has a distinct look and method of hooking up with the machine. Additionally, each kind is utilized for a particular purpose. Modern connection systems possess different connectors (e.g. modular connectors, motherboard connectors, SATA connectors, etc.).

Usually, a power supply has a two-position sliding switch on its rear section. Here are three of the most popular switch options: (1) 120 – 140, (2) 110 – 120, and (3) 115 – 230. You can use this switch to control the voltage level of the power supply.

Power Connectors

These days, the connectors used in power supplies have varying characteristics. However, there are some connectors that you can only find in old power supplies. This part of the book will focus on the different types of power connectors used in computers.

The Classic Connectors

This category is composed of old connectors and those used in the first IBM personal computer.

- The AT System Connectors – This subcategory involves all the original connectors attached to old motherboards.

- Standard Power Connectors – In general, you should use these connectors to power various kinds of disk drives. Some people refer to these connectors as "Molex."

- Floppy Drive Connectors – These connectors are ideal in supplying power to small devices (e.g. floppy disk drives). These are the smallest and flattest connectors available today.

The Modern Connectors

Modern parts have surpassed the capacities of older power connectors. The standard connectors and floppy drive connectors still exist, but AT system connectors are no longer available. Additionally, many manufacturers have developed better alternatives. Here are some of the modern power connectors:

- ATX Connectors – These connectors provide power to ATX motherboards. They use a single connector to deliver the voltage needed by the device. According to computer technicians, an ATX connector is simpler and easier to use than AT ones.

- ATX12V Connectors – With the emergence of new processors and computer systems, manufacturers had to develop power supplies that can provide varying voltages. This situation resulted to the creation of ATX12V, which is an ATX connector that has 2 extra wires. The first wire is a 6-pin connector that adds 3.3V and 5V leads to the current power. The second one, however, is a 4-pin connector that adds two 12V leads to the supplied power.

- EPS12V Connectors – These connectors have 8-pin wires that can supply up to four 12V leads.

How to Replace a Power Supply?

Replacing a computer's power supply is not an easy task. First, you have to make sure that the power supply's capabilities match the needs of your machine. For example, you shouldn't buy ATX connectors if you are using an AT motherboard.

Next, you need to consider the power supply's physical size when choosing one. If you'll purchase a typical ATX power supply, you'll have problems inserting it into the small case of a micro-ATX computer. In this situation, you must look for power supplies that can fit into the case of your computer.

How to Remove a Power Supply

- Make sure that the computer is disconnected from its power source.

- Remove the system unit's cover. By doing so, you'll expose the internal parts of your computer.

- Locate the power supply and disconnect all of its wiring harnesses.

- Remove everything that can obstruct the extraction of the power supply. With this approach, you are making sure that the extraction process will be quick and smooth.

- Unscrew the power supply. You have to be extremely careful in doing this task. The last thing you want to do is unscrew other computer parts. Additionally, support the power supply using your hand as you unscrew it from the case. Since the power supply is heavy, it may destroy computer parts that it will fall onto.

- Pull out the power supply from the computer's case.

Real World Example: Power Connectors

During the 90s, Toby Skandler established a computer sales and repair shop. In those days, you could set up computers from scratch, sell them with a high markup, and still be considered as a cheaper option than branded systems.

A certain customer was extremely conscious to prices. In those times, floppy drives were both necessary and expensive. Customers who wanted to save some money chose cheap floppy drive models. This particular customer was purchasing 45 PCs. Knowing that he will be paying a large amount of money, the customer decided to lower his invoice amount by acquiring the cheapest floppy drives available.

The cheap drives are identical to the pricey ones, from the user's perspective, but the differences appeared while the technicians were setting up the computer systems. The manufacturer saved money in producing power connectors. Where typical manufacturers produce a case to hold the power supply's connector, this manufacturer didn't care if the connector's pins were sticking out.

Unlike other types of power connectors, the ones used for floppy drives can be installed upside down if the computer's case doesn't have a holder for them. Upside-down connectors cause no issues when they are connected to the computer system or when the machine is turned on. However, they burn the floppy drive's 5V circuit board each time the computer was booted up. The burning plastic gave off an undesirable and alarming smell.

When one of the technicians activated one of those floppy drives, Mr. Toby Skandler learned a valuable lesson: don't plug the power connectors upside down. This lesson was so simple and clear that everyone in the shop smelled it. Fortunately, Mr. Skandler's team only lost one floppy drive. The shop could've experienced a huge financial loss if the technicians weren't careful.

Chapter 7: Customized Computer Systems

Some situations require specific computer capabilities. For example, some small laptops are excellent in terms of portability but are useless when creating mathematical models of complicated systems. The supercomputers that can accomplish this task require constant assembly and disassembly each time they are transported. These examples, although extreme, highlight the benefits offered by customized computer systems.

This chapter will focus on the most popular custom configurations for computers. Study this material carefully since it can help you pass the A+ certification exam.

CAD/CAM and Graphic Design Computers

Computers used for designing graphical content put heavy loads of data on the following areas:

- Maximized Ram

- CPU Enhancements

- Video Enhancements

Let's discuss each of these areas:

Maximized Ram

These computers utilize modern video systems. However, they still need adequate RAM to hold the computer's instructions while performing their tasks. Graphics programs are inherently RAM and CPU hungry. If you want to improve your computer's performance, you have to maximize the volume of RAM that is accessible to the OS and CPU.

CPU Enhancements

Sometimes, you need to use a powerful CPU. In some cases, however, you must use multiple weaker CPUs to complete separate tasks quickly. Most of today's computers have one or both of these characteristics. Nevertheless, some computers with single and weak CPUs exist in the market. That means you have to assess the machine's purpose when selecting its CPU profile.

CAD/CAM (i.e. computer-aided design/computer-aided manufacturing) and graphic design computers are machines that can work on similar yet distinctive tasks. CAD/CAM computers help engineers and architects in creating documentations, such as 2D and 3D blueprints. Graphic design computers, on the other hand, help book publishers in creating excellent copy composed of professional-looking text and images.

These computers place heavy loads on their processors. Computers with mediocre processors may experience problems when running graphics-intensive programs; thus, CAD/CAM and graphic design systems require above-average CPUs.

- CAD/CAM Computers – These computers turn the user's concepts into actual designs. Architects and engineers use these designs to produce three-dimensional models. The programs required for such tasks need a large quantity of processor cycles while rendering the designs on a monitor.

- Graphic Design Computers – These machines work on different shapes and colors. In general, shapes and colors put a lot of strain on the computer's video, RAM and CPU components.

Video Enhancements

This is a basic requirement for CAD/CAM and graphic design systems. You have to include graphic adapters with better GPUs (graphics processing units) and extra RAM to make sure that your computer can keep up with the demands of graphics-intensive software. Such pieces of software put an unacceptable strain on the RAM and CPU of computers; thus, you will experience technical difficulties if your machine doesn't have sufficient RAM and specialized processors.

Video/Audio Editing Computers

People who edit multimedia content need computers that excel in:

- Specialized Drives

- Specialized Audio

- Video Enhancements

This section assumes that the user employs NLE (i.e. Nonlinear Editing) schemes for visual content. In NLE, the content to be modified is stored in a local drive. NLE needs computers with high RAM and storage space. Although you can benefit from RAM maximization, the three aspects given above are more important in attaining great computer performance.

Specialized drives

Computers designed for graphics editing benefit from separating the drive that holds the OS and programs from the one that contains the edited files. With this setup, the drives of your computer won't have to perform lots of multitasking. If you are using the system drive as the input source in encoding video materials, utilize the data drive to store your outputs.

Aside from using different drives for storing system and media files, you have to make sure that your media storage is fast and large. Computer experts recommend SATA drives that run at 7200 rpm to people who want to edit audio and video files. Inefficient storage systems can lead to delays and slow playback.

Specialized Audio

The audio controllers you see today are similar to the original devices used in the 80s. These controllers still rely on analog codecs with plain 2-channel arrangements. If you want to get great performance from your machine, you need to have seven to eight audio channels.

Most motherboards available in the market have built-in analog audio devices. Although analog audio can give acceptable performance, professional sound editors prefer digital audio.

Important Note: In certain cases, you have to install add-on adapters before you can use digital audio in your workstation.

Video Enhancements

Video/Audio editing computers benefit from high-performance video subsystems. However, you shouldn't focus on these subsystems when improving your machines.

You will gain the most benefit from graphics adapters with multiple interfaces for video. Many computer stores sell this kind of adapter, although you may still find expensive ones with a single interface. Avoid single-interface graphics adapters since these are not ideal for Video/Audio editing systems.

To ensure excellent performance, look for adapters that support CUDA and OpenCL. CUDA is a computing architecture used by Nvidia (a popular manufacturer of graphics adapters) to facilitate quick and easy processes. OpenCL (i.e. Open Computing Language) is another computing architecture that you can use across different platforms.

Virtualization Computers

System virtualization gained unbelievable popularity in the IT industry. This technology has given birth to large companies. Basically, virtualization helps people in establishing new workstations and network servers. This part of the book will explain the basic requirements of computers that host virtualized systems.

A virtualization computer must surpass the capabilities of typical computers and servers in the following aspects:

- RAM Maximization

- CPU Improvements

You may be required to increase the storage capacity of the computer, depending on the guest systems that it will host. However, since this situation rarely happens, drive capacity is not a major requirement for virtualization computers.

VMs (i.e. virtual machines) that run on another computer look like they have their own system resources. A cursory look at the Device Manager section of the OS tells you that the VM can run without relying on external systems. This is false, however. To function properly, a virtual machine must obtain the following resources from its host:

- System Memory

- CPU Cycles

- Network Bandwidth

- Storage Space

RAM Maximization

While creating virtual machines, you have to determine the amount of RAM the hosted systems will need. Keep in mind that the installation requirements of an OS on a regular machine also apply to virtual computers.

The VM won't use the RAM assigned to it if it's turned off. That means the virtualization computer (i.e. the host) can use the additional RAM in doing other tasks. If the VM is on, however, the assigned RAM is completely useless to the host. Because of this, you have to equip your virtualization computer with enough RAM to manage its own processes and those of the hosted systems.

When working with VMs, imagine that you are working on multiple computers that run on a single OS. Provide extra RAM to each VM to make sure that it works along perfectly.

Consider the total amount of RAM when configuring the virtualization computer. Often, this leads to the maximization of the RAM available in the machine. The maximum RAM that you can use depends on three things:

- The width of the processor's address-bus

- The maximum RAM that the OS can support

- The maximum RAM that the motherboard can handle

Consider the factors listed above when choosing a virtualization computer. Because of OS limitations, it is advisable to use x64 versions, instead of x86 versions, and server-side versions instead of client-side versions.

CPU Improvements

You need to equip your virtualization computers with multiple CPUs. This is because all active operating systems (both actual and virtual) require this resource. If you don't have enough processors, the hosted systems will experience lags and/or crashes.

Operating systems can treat each core in multicore processors as separate units. That means you can set up one virtual CPU from each core. You can increase the number of CPU cycles assigned to the hosted systems by installing several multicore CPUs into your virtualization computer.

Real World Example: Virtualization Computers

The virtualization technology attracts countless businesses and organizations across the globe. This technology offers cost-effectiveness and environment-friendliness, two things that every business needs. Because of this, a medium-sized company decided to implement their own version of system virtualization. The manager asked the IT department to remove the KVM switch. Then, he asked the technicians to redesign the server room so that only a single computer handles all of the network processes.

The IT people did what they're supposed to do. They selected the organization's best server and generated 5 VMs. The hard disk's capacity was enough to handle the needs of the host and the five virtual machines. The technicians also provided a lot of RAM to the virtualization computer. They didn't modify the host's CPU, however, since it was powerful enough to handle all of the processes.

After installing the necessary programs, the technicians tested the virtualized network. The host computer booted perfectly. The first VM also worked well – the technicians were able to access it throughout the network. The VM handled requests perfectly and showed excellent performance.

The second VM, however, showed that the manager and the IT people missed an important point. The RAM and CPU resources in the network were sufficient for the host and a single VM. When another VM was turned on, the network suffered from an untenable RAM and CPU depletion.

Fortunately, the technicians were skilled and knowledgeable. They replaced the host's motherboard with a new one. The new motherboard had two quad-core Xeon processors. Then, the technicians maximized the available RAM based on the motherboard's specifications. These changes resulted to an excellent network with five VMs. Each virtual machine showed great performance statistics.

Chapter 8: Computer Networks

These days, networks play an important role in the IT industry. Almost all businesses implement a computer network to facilitate their daily processes. Wireless networks have become extremely popular among households in the past few years. Before, you'll find one or two wireless networks if you will run a search using a laptop. Today, you may find 10-12, depending on your location.

In this chapter, you'll learn about the basics of computer networking. This material will explain how networks work, how data travels across different devices, and the different kinds of network that you will encounter. Several years ago, you can become a good technician just by focusing on a single computer. Today, however, you have to know how to troubleshoot software and/or hardware problems on entire networks.

The Principles of Networking

Stand-alone PCs that were introduced back in the 70s allowed users to create and store files (e.g. documents, spreadsheets, presentations, etc.). These computers are more than enough to meet the needs of personal users and small businesses. However, large businesses and organizations need more computing capabilities than what stand-alone machines can provide. Single PCs are not enough because:

- Their storage capacity is too small.

- They should have a local printer to print documents.

- They can't share documents quickly. For instance, the users need to use removable disks just to share files with other computers. IT experts refer to this setup as "sneakernet."

To solve these problems, the concept of networking was born. A network connects two or more computers to facilitate easy communication and file distribution. Networking became a huge hit: the entire IT industry is now relying on it. These days, companies can improve their overall efficiency and productivity by linking their departments internally.

Computer networks allow several machines to connect to each other's files and resources. For instance, if you are in a network, you don't have to connect a printer to each computer. Rather, you may link a printer to one of the machines (or straight to the network) and allow other machines to utilize that resource.

The Basics of Networking

Many people consider modern networking as a plug-and-play procedure. You can detect and join networks using wireless network adapters: in just a few seconds, you can surf the net, send emails, download songs, etc.

Obviously, some networks are more complex than others. Establishing your own network involves various configurations – a single mistake can result to undesirable results.

Before learning how to establish a network, you should know how networks work. The following section will help you understand the basic aspects of networking.

Different Types of Networks

Networks are divided into four types:

- LANs (i.e. Local Area Networks) – This is the ideal network type for computers inside a single room or building.

- PANs (Personal Area Networks) – Individuals who work alone use this network in setting up their computer systems. PANs rely on Bluetooth-compatible devices to share files and resources.

- WANs (Wide Area Networks) – This is the expanded version of local networks. In general, a WAN allows users to connect to machines outside the local area. WANs also help in transmitting resources to different locations. You may think of a WAN as interconnected LANs.

- MANs (Metropolitan Area Networks) – These networks are larger than LANs but smaller than WANs. IT experts say that MANs are networks that span a city or a huge campus.

Major Parts of a Network

You can create a network just by connecting two or more computers. However, in real life, networks are more complex than that. When troubleshooting networks, you have to look at the following components:

- Clients – A client is a computer on which the users perform their tasks (e.g. sending emails, creating designs, reading files, etc.). Clients are ordinary computers that got linked to a network, allowing them to use additional resources.

- Servers – This kind of component comes in different sizes and shapes. Servers are considered as main components of any network. They allow users to access resources stored in any part of the network. They also help client computers in finding the necessary files or programs.

- Resources – In computer networking, a resource is an object that can be accessed and utilized by the client or the server. This category includes a wide range of objects, but the most important ones are:

  o Programs

  o File Access and Disk Storage

  o Peripherals (e.g. printers)

Resource Accessibility

Modern networks utilize one of the following access models: client-server and peer-to-peer. You have to choose the right access model if you want to get excellent network performance. The following questions will help you determine the best model for your network:

- What is the network's size?

- Does the network need high-level security?

- What hardware or software are you planning to use within the network?

- Does the network need constant administration?

- What is your budget?

- Do you have to train the network technicians further?

You can't just link computers together and expect to get great network performance. You need to do some careful planning before establishing a computer network. This approach helps you in ensuring that the network will satisfy your current and future needs. As a network designer, you must strive for great performance and minimal administration.

Topologies

The term "topology" refers to the layout of the network. When planning and installing networks, you should select the best topology for your project. Each kind has distinct costs, ease of use and "fault tolerance" (i.e. how the layout handles issues such as power failures). Here are the most popular network topologies:

- Star – In this layout, the network devices are connected to a core device known as a "hub." The hub allows network designers to add workstations quickly and easily. If a client experiences technical problems, the other members of the network won't be affected. If the hub goes down, however, the whole network will crash. This is the reason why IT experts refer to hubs as "points of failure."

- Bus – This is the simplest topology that you can use. Here, a cable is connected to each client computer. The computers share the same address and data path.

- Mesh – This layout has the most complicated design among all network topologies. Here, you have to connect each computer to the other computers. Since this topology involves complex cabling, you won't find this in PANs and LANs.

- Ring – To achieve this topology, you have to connect each machine to two other machines. Create a circle using the connected computers. This way, network resources can travel from one computer to another just by following a single direction.

- Hybrid – Basically, a hybrid topology is a combination of two or more topologies. Large companies normally use this topology to meet their complex network requirements. Since this approach involves the use of multiple layouts, it is considered as the most expensive topology.

The Rules Related to Communication

The computers within a network should know how to communicate with each other. To enable communications throughout a network, the computers must use a single language (known as protocol). Just like any other language, protocols have rules that must be followed to ensure proper communication.

Computers can't think for themselves. That means you have to set standards to keep intra-network communications clear. Various standards are currently available – use the one that works best for your network.

The OSI Model, known as the backbone of all networks, is one of the most useful communication frameworks available today.

How to Identify Network Hardware?

Computers need to use pieces of hardware to communicate with each other. Each computer within a network should have a network adapter. Often, the technician also needs to link the machines using a cable connection. Additionally, the computers may require connectivity devices to enable peer-to-peer and/or client-server communications.

NICs

NICs (i.e. network interface cards) provide the interface between the computers and the network cabling. These interface cards prepare, send and control data. They can also accept and convert data into a language that the computer can understand.

These days, NICs are available in different shapes and sizes. You can distinguish NICs by checking their bus type and the network they are designed for. Here are the factors you have to consider when choosing NICs for your computers:

- Compatibility – Make sure that the NIC matches the bus type/s of your computer. If your computer has multiple bus types, choose an NIC that works for the fastest bus type. This trick is extremely important in network servers. If you won't use it, the NIC can slow the whole network down.

- Configuration - Each NIC should have a unique MAC address. If two or more NICs share the same MAC address, they won't be able to interact. Because of this, the IEEE (i.e. Institute of Electrical and Electronics Engineers) has set a standard for MAC addresses and gives groups of these addresses to interface card manufacturers. The manufacturers "burn" these MAC addresses onto their products. This way, they can make sure that each NIC has a unique MAC address.

- Performance – Look for NICs that offer excellent network performance and minimal processing time for data transfers. Get the fastest interface card available for the network you are using.

- Drivers – For NICs to work, you should install the correct device drivers into your computers. These device drivers interact with network adapters and redirectors.

- Data Control – Before two machines can exchange data, their interface cards should agree on the following:

  o The data frame's maximum size

  o The volume of information transmitted before confirming the process

  o The time to be allotted between data transmissions

  o The speed of the data transmission

  o The length of time the computers must wait before giving confirmation

Cables

Your network must have a medium that can transfer data from one computer to the next. Computer users refer to this medium as the "cable." Basically, cables deliver the data to its proper destination. Here are the three main types of cables:

1. Coaxial – This cable has a copper conductor in its center. A jacket (usually made of plastic) surrounds the conductor. To provide better security, cable manufacturers cover their products with a metal shield.

2. Twisted-Pair – Network designers love this cable because it is cheap and flexible. If you'll dissect a twisted-pair cable, you'll find multiple pairs of twisted wires placed inside insulating jackets.

3. Fiber-Optic – IT experts consider this as the best cable for computer networking. A fiber-optic cable consists of a fiber (usually made of plastic or glass) that is surrounded by a rubber coating. With this kind of cable, you can transfer 10Gbps of data to a computer that is several miles away. Since it uses light to send information, it can resist wiretapping and electrical interference.

The Tools Used for Cabling

Here are the tools that you can use in troubleshooting network cables:

- Crimper – This tool can help you in attaching connectors into your cables. You can also use it to strip and cut wires.

- Multimeter – This measuring tool is extremely versatile. You can use it to measure current, resistance and voltage present on a cable. There is a wide range of multi-meters currently available in the market: from $10 ones to those that cost $1000+.

- Cable Tester – This tool is an important part of any technician's toolbox. Often, you have to use a cable tester before installing any cable. Obviously, you can still test your cables after installing them.

- Toner Probe – You can use this tool to trace wires from one place to another. Since toner probes are excellent wire trackers, some people refer to them as "foxes and hounds."

- Punch-Down Tool – This tool allows you to connect wire ends securely. Technicians use a punch-down tool to arrange messy cables.

- Loopback Plug – With this tool, you can test the network adapter's ability to transmit data. You just have to plug this tool into the network interface card to perform the test. In just a few seconds, you'll know if the NIC is functioning or not.

The Components of a Network

You may use cables to link multiple computers. However, most networks are more complex than three-computer setups. Use different networking devices to make sure that your computers can communicate and share resources properly. These networking devices provide network connectivity, improve the network's size, and give auxiliary functions to network users.

In this part of the book, you'll learn about the networking components that you will encounter in the CompTIA A+ exam. Let's divide these components into two categories: connectivity devices and auxiliary devices.

Connectivity Devices

Connectivity devices allow you to establish large computer networks. With a connectivity device, you can forget about the limitations imposed by LANs or PANs. Here are the most popular connectivity devices:

- Modems – This is the device you need if you want to create networks using standard phone lines and dial-up connections.

- Hubs – You can use this tool to connect multiple computers together. A hub is a simple tool that doesn't have any form of AI (artificial intelligence). It simply repeats the signals it receives. Because of this, some people use the term "multiple repeater" when referring to a hub.

- Bridges – This connectivity device segregates network traffic. It prevents traffic from going to network segments where no recipients are available. Bridges are "smarter" than hubs. However, bridges cannot transmit data to different networks at the same time.

- Access Points – Basically, these are points that allow you to connect to the network. These days, however, people use this term when referring to WAPs (i.e. wireless access points). A WAP lets people connect to the network wirelessly.

- Routers – This connectivity device possesses advance intelligence and networking capability. Even the most basic router can link various networks together and identify the quickest path for data transmission.

- Switches – These devices analyze incoming data packets and forward them to the correct port. By setting up a virtual link between senders and receivers, a switch can greatly improve the performance of a computer network.

Auxiliary Devices

An auxiliary device provides additional features to a network. It helps users in completing their tasks and protecting the network from hackers. The list below shows the frequently used auxiliary devices:

- Firewall – This is a piece of software that guards the network from viruses and hacking attacks. IT experts consider firewalls as the most important auxiliary device currently available. In most cases, network admins also use firewalls to block undesirable websites (e.g. porn sites).

- NAS (i.e. Network-Attached Storage) – This is a special device that serves as additional storage for the entire network. You may think of NASs as storage devices that are linked straight to the network.

- VoIP (i.e. Voice over Internet Protocol) – VoIP is a technology that transmits voice signals through the internet. Excellent VoIP systems allow people to send voice, video and data simultaneously.

- Internet Appliance – This is a special device that provides internet connectivity. You can use it to complete online activities such as emailing and web surfing.

Chapter 9: The TCP/IP Protocol

This chapter will focus on TCP/IP, the most popular networking protocol today. This protocol is so effective that it is used in homes, businesses and other networks. Actually, TCP/IP is the protocol used by websites to connect with their visitors.

What is TCP/IP?

Protocols are rules that regulate digital communication, similar to the languages of humans. Of all the protocols available these days, the one you have to understand is TCP/IP. Actually, the TCP/IP suite contains various protocols that function together to provide network connectivity. Because of this, TCP/IP is the only protocol included in the CompTIA A+ exam.

The Structure of TCP/IP

The structure of the TCP/IP suite follows the DOD (i.e. Department of Defense) model, which was the brainchild of the United States Department of Defense. This model contains four layers: (1) process/application, (2) host-to-host, (3) internet, and (4) network access.

The Process/Application layer holds most of the protocols within TCP/IP. The Host-to-Host layer, on the other hand, only has two protocols. The internet layer contains some of the most important protocols in the TCP/IP suite. The final layer does not hold any protocols. It simply defines the kind of access (e.g. Ethernet) used in the network.

Let's discuss the protocols inside each layer:

The Protocols in the Process/Application Layer

- Dynamic Host Configuration Protocol – This protocol, also known as DHCP, assigns dynamic configuration data (e.g. IP address) to the computers within the network. You can streamline network administration by distributing IP addresses through DHCP.

- Domain Name System – This protocol resolves hostnames to their corresponding IP addresses. For instance, let's assume that you want to visit the Google website using Google Chrome. Your computer should identify the IP address of the webserver that hosts www.google.com to establish a connection. Using the DNS protocol, the machine resolves the www.google.com URL to a specific IP address.

- File Transfer Protocol – People use this protocol to transfer files. That means you can use it to upload and/or download files from any computer within the network. However, you can't use this protocol to launch applications from a remote location.

- Internet Message Access Protocol – This protocol allows you to download the messages from your email service provider.

- Lightweight Directory Access Protocol – You can use this protocol to provide directory services. This protocol, also known as LDAP, can access data stored in databases or directories linked to the network.

- Remote Desktop Protocol – Microsoft, one of the giants in the IT industry, developed this protocol. Basically, this protocol allows you to control machines that are far away from you.

- Telnet – IT experts refer to telnet as "terminal emulation protocol." While using Telnet, you can access another computer and view it as another window on your monitor. This protocol allows you to manipulate remote computers as if you are sitting in front of them.

- Hypertext Transfer Protocol – This protocol controls the interaction between clients and webservers. It is also the protocol you use when surfing the internet.

- Hypertext Transfer Protocol Secure – This protocol, also called HTTPS, uses SSL (i.e. secure sockets layer) or TLS (i.e. transport layer security) to transmit data securely. Online merchants utilize this protocol when handling the financial information (e.g. credit card details) of their customers.

- Secure File Transfer Protocol – You can use this protocol to transfer files using an encrypted connection.

- Server Message Block – This protocol, which was also developed by Microsoft, allows you to share files, printers and other resources throughout a network. Basically, it is an improved version of FTP.

- Simple Mail Transfer Protocol – Mail clients (e.g. Microsoft Outlook) use this protocol to send emails. Computer users refer to it as "push protocol" since it is only designed for sending electronic messages.

- Simple Network Management Protocol – With this protocol, you can collect and analyze information related to the network's performance.

The Protocols in the Host-to-Host Layer

This layer involves two simple protocols: TCP and UDP. Both of these protocols allow you to connect multiple network hosts together. The main difference between TCP and UDP is that the former delivers data packets through data acknowledgements and virtual circuits and the latter doesn't. This is the reason why network admins use the term "connection-oriented protocol" when referring to TCP and "connectionless protocol" when referring to UDP. Since UDP doesn't involve any direct connection, it is clearly faster than TCP. However, the difference is so tiny (you can only measure it in milliseconds) you won't really notice it while accessing the network.

The Protocols in the Internet Layer

This layer contains a major protocol (i.e. Internet Protocol) and some minor protocols. The Internet Protocol, also called IP, helps in managing network addresses and sending information from one location to another.

The minor protocols in this layer are the following:

- Internet Control Message Protocol – This protocol helps the network in sending error messages.

- Address Resolution Protocol – Computers use this protocol to resolve IP addresses to MAC addresses that are pre-installed into NICs.

- Reverse Address Resolution Protocol – With this protocol, a computer can resolve MAC addresses to their corresponding IP addresses.

IP Addresses

IP addresses have two parts: the network part and the host part. The former always comes first before the latter. Because of this structure, the network part may have different lengths. For instance, in a 32-bit system, some computers may assign 8 bits to the network part and the remaining bits to the host part. Other computers may assign 24 bits to the network part and give the remaining bits to the host part.

Here are the principles you need to keep in mind when dealing with an IP address:

- Each IP address must be unique. No two computers can share the same IP address.

- An IP address can't be all ones or zeroes.

- In routed networks (e.g. the internet), each network should have a unique address.

Real World Example: HTTP and HTTPS

These days, you can buy almost anything online. However, you should never give your personal and/or financial information to unsecure websites. Here are the things you need to remember:

Look for websites with HTTPS in their address. If the website's address (also called URL) begins with HTTP, there's a possibility that someone will steal your personal and/or financial information. HTTP sends data to webservers without any encryption. That means anyone can view the information and use it for malicious purposes. HTTPS, on the other hand, encrypts the data before sending it to the site's webserver. That means hackers will have a hard time getting your information.

To have HTTPS in its URL, a website should get a Secure Socket Layer certificate from a reputable website service provider. Getting an SSL certificate is not easy. The company or organization has to submit certain requirements and follow strict guidelines. This way, confidential data can travel across the internet securely.

Conclusion

Thank you again for downloading this book!

I hope this book was able to help you to prepare for the CompTIA A+ tests.

The next step is to reread this book and use other information sources. That way, you can increase your chances of passing the exam.

Finally, if you enjoyed this book, please take the time to share your thoughts and post a review on Amazon. It'd be greatly appreciated!

Thank you and good luck!